I Can Thank God

Published by Standard Publishing, Cincinnati, Ohio. www.standardpub.com. Copyright © 2001, 2007 Standard Publishing. All rights reserved. Happy Day logo and trade dress are trademarks of Standard Publishing. Illustrated by Robin Boyer. All Scripture quotations, unless otherwise indicated, are taken from the *International Children's Bible*®, copyright © 1986, 1988, 1999, 2005 by Thomas Nelson, Inc. All rights reserved. Used by permission. Reproducible: Permission is granted to reproduce these pages for ministry purposes only—not for resale.

ISBN 978-0-7847-2057-8

14 13 12 11 10 09 08 07   7 6 5 4 3 2 1

Standard®
PUBLISHING
Bringing The Word to Life

Cincinnati, Ohio

**Celebrate the harvest! "The Lord will give his goodness.
And the land will give its crops."** Psalm 85:12

Remember last spring? We planted tiny seeds.
We wanted them to grow into a great harvest.

God helped our plants grow, so we have plenty to eat.

I will honor God by thanking him.

The bright red apples are ready to be harvested.

Grandma makes apple cider. Yum!

"Thank the Lord because he is good." *Psalm 106:1*

In the fall, leaves turn shades of red, yellow, and orange.

The leaves fall down, and we rake them into big piles.

Each fall, we go to the harvest festival at our church.

We play fun games and have a costume contest!

**We eat popcorn and caramel apples
and other yummy fall treats.**

For Thanksgiving, we decorate our home with dried corn, fall wreaths, and scarecrows.

Thanksgiving dinner is a feast of all the good food God has given to us.

We say, "Thank you, God, for your care!"